by Iain Gray

PUBLISHING

WRITING *to* REMEMBER

Lang**Syne**

PUBLISHING

WRITING *to* REMEMBER

79 Main Street, Newtongrange,
Midlothian EH22 4NA
Tel: 0131 344 0414   Fax: 0845 075 6085
E-mail: info@lang-syne.co.uk
www.langsyneshop.co.uk

Design by Dorothy Meikle
Printed by Printwell Ltd
© Lang Syne Publishers Ltd 2017

ISBN 978-1-85217-596-2

Scott

MOTTO:
For King and country
(and)
All good or nothing.

CREST:
A demi-griffin.

NAME variations include:
Scot.

Chapter one:

The origins of popular surnames

by George Forbes and Iain Gray

If you don't know where you came from, you won't know where you're going is a frequently quoted observation and one that has a particular resonance today when there has been a marked upsurge in interest in genealogy, with increasing numbers of people curious to trace their family roots.

Main sources for genealogical research include census returns and official records of births, marriages and deaths – and the key to unlocking the detail they contain is obviously a family surname, one that has been 'inherited' and passed from generation to generation.

No matter our station in life, we all have a surname – but it was not until about the middle of the fourteenth century that the practice of being identified by a particular surname became commonly established throughout the British Isles.

Previous to this, it was normal for a person to be identified through the use of only a forename.

But as population gradually increased and there were many more people with the same forename, surnames were adopted to distinguish one person, or community, from another.

Many common English surnames are patronymic in origin, meaning they stem from the forename of one's father – with 'Johnson,' for example, indicating 'son of John.'

It was the Normans, in the wake of their eleventh century conquest of Anglo-Saxon England, a pivotal moment in the nation's history, who first brought surnames into usage – although it was a gradual process.

For the Normans, these were names initially based on the title of their estates, local villages and chateaux in France to distinguish and identify these landholdings.

Such grand descriptions also helped enhance the prestige of these warlords and generally glorify their lofty positions high above the humble serfs slaving away below in the pecking order who had only single names, often with Biblical connotations as in Pierre and Jacques.

The only descriptive distinctions among the peasantry concerned their occupations, like 'Pierre the swineherd' or 'Jacques the ferryman.'

Roots of surnames that came into usage in England not only included Norman-French, but also Old French, Old Norse, Old English, Middle English, German, Latin, Greek, Hebrew and the Gaelic languages of the Celts.

The Normans themselves were originally Vikings, or 'Northmen', who raided, colonised and eventually settled down around the French coastline.

The had sailed up the Seine in their longboats in 900AD under their ferocious leader Rollo and ruled the roost in north eastern France before sailing over to conquer England in 1066 under Duke William of Normandy – better known to posterity as William the Conqueror, or King William I of England.

Granted lands in the newly-conquered England, some of their descendants later acquired territories in Wales, Scotland and Ireland – taking not only their own surnames, but also the practice of adopting a surname, with them.

But it was in England where Norman rule and custom first impacted, particularly in relation to the adoption of surnames.

This is reflected in the famous *Domesday Book*, a massive survey of much of England and Wales, ordered by William I, to determine who owned what, what it was worth and therefore how much they were liable to pay in taxes to the voracious Royal Exchequer.

Completed in 1086 and now held in the National Archives in Kew, London, 'Domesday' was an Old English word meaning 'Day of Judgement.'

This was because, in the words of one contemporary chronicler, "its decisions, like those of the Last Judgement, are unalterable."

It had been a requirement of all those English landholders – from the richest to the poorest – that they identify themselves for the purposes of the survey and for future reference by means of a surname.

This is why the *Domesday Book*, although written in Latin as was the practice for several centuries with both civic and ecclesiastical records, is an invaluable source for the early appearance of a wide range of English surnames.

Several of these names were coined in connection with occupations.

These include Baker and Smith, while Cooks, Chamberlains, Constables and Porters were to be found carrying out duties in large medieval households.

The church's influence can be found in names such as Bishop, Friar and Monk while the popular name of Bennett derives from the late fifth to mid-sixth century Saint Benedict, founder of the Benedictine order of monks.

The early medical profession is represented by Barber, while businessmen produced names that include Merchant and Sellers.

Down at the village watermill, the names that cropped up included Millar/Miller, Walker and Fuller, while other self-explanatory trades included Cooper, Tailor, Mason and Wright.

Even the scenery was utilised as in Moor, Hill, Wood and Forrest – while the hunt and the chase supplied names that include Hunter, Falconer, Fowler and Fox.

Colours are also a source of popular surnames, as in Black, Brown, Gray/Grey, Green and White, and would have denoted the colour of the clothing the person habitually wore or, apart from the obvious exception of 'Green', one's hair colouring or even complexion.

The surname Red developed into Reid, while

Blue was rare and no-one wanted to be associated with yellow.

Rather self-important individuals took surnames that include Goodman and Wiseman, while physical attributes crept into surnames such as Small and Little.

Many families proudly boast the heraldic device known as a Coat of Arms, as featured on our front cover.

The central motif of the Coat of Arms would originally have been what was borne on the shield of a warrior to distinguish himself from others on the battlefield.

Not featured on the Coat of Arms, but high-lighted on page three, is the family motto and related crest – with the latter frequently different from the central motif.

Adding further variety to the rich cultural heritage that is represented by surnames is the appearance in recent times in lists of the 100 most common names found in England of ones that include Khan, Patel and Singh – names that have proud roots in the vast sub-continent of India.

Echoes of a far distant past can still be found in our surnames and they can be borne with pride in commemoration of our forebears.

Chapter two:

Honours and distinction

Although a surname of specifically Scottish origin, 'Scott' is nevertheless ranked 42nd in some lists of the 100 most popular names found in England today.

Derived from the Latin 'Scotti', it denoted the Celts of Ireland, some of whom settled on the western seaboard of Scotland from about the late fifth century and later gave their name to what became 'Scotland.'

But those who would take the Scott name were not confined to the northern kingdom, where their main territory was present day Jedburgh, in Roxburghshire, in the Scottish Borders.

Interaction with England meant that many were to be found there, and one of the reasons for this goes back to the reign from 1124 to 1153 of King David I of Scotland who, impressed by Anglo-Norman customs and manners, invited many to settle in his native land.

Among them, for example, were the Bruces – whose most famous son was the great warrior king Robert the Bruce.

These Anglo-Norman families also retained their original estates in England, and this meant that up until the bitter thirteenth and fourteenth century Wars of Independence there was a highly fluid interaction between both nations.

With the outbreak of the Wars of Independence, many were faced with conflicting loyalties – only too well aware that support for Scotland's cause would lead to the loss of their English estates.

This was a fear that England's Edward I, known as 'The Hammer of the Scots', exploited to the full – buying the loyalty of wavering Scots nobles by guaranteeing them the retention of the English land-holdings in addition to further rewards.

One prominent family of the Scott name came to be settled in Kent, known today as 'the garden of England.'

To determine how this may have come about, we have to travel back through the dim mists of time to 1290 when, following the death of the young Margaret, Maid of Norway and heiress to Alexander III of Scotland, John Balliol became a competitor for the Scottish crown.

There were several other competitors, in

what became known as the Great Cause, but Balliol's main rival was Robert Bruce, 5th Lord of Annandale and grandfather of the future King Robert the Bruce.

The Scottish nobility had asked Edward I to arbitrate in the matter of the succession to the Scottish crown and, through his powerful influence, Balliol was pronounced the rightful heir and duly inaugurated as such in November of 1292.

Balliol, born in about 1249, was the son of John, 5th Baron Balliol, Lord of Barnard Castle in England's Co. Durham, and Dervorguilla of Galloway, in Scotland, and granddaughter of the Earl of Huntingdon.

Through this, he had extensive holdings not only in Scotland but also in England, including the estate of Hitchin, in Herefordshire.

But, despite his kingship and great wealth, his life was blighted.

Edward I had haughtily declared himself Lord Paramount of Scotland and Balliol was accordingly treated as a mere vassal, owing fealty to the English monarch.

Deeply rankled with this humiliating state of affairs, a number of Scottish nobles concluded an alliance with France – the Auld Alliance – in July of

1295. Edward's response was to invade the northern kingdom.

As his forces wreaked fire and havoc across Scotland, Balliol was forced to abdicate in July of the following year and, on Edward's orders, the proud arms of Scotland were formally torn from his tunic – giving the hapless Balliol the nickname of 'Toom Tabard', or 'Empty Coat.'

Imprisoned for a time in the Tower of London, he was later allowed to retire to his French estates in Picardy, and it was here that he died in 1314.

It was through one of his close relatives – the precise relationship is not known with any degree of certainty – that the prominent Kentish family of Scott descend.

This was William Balliol, also known as William Balliol le (the) Scot – and it is from 'le Scott' that the 'Scott' or 'Scot' name may have been adopted by the family.

His background is a tangled genealogical weave. But what is known is that he was a close relation of Alexander de Balliol, Lord of Chilham, Kent, and who died in 1309.

William Balliol's date of birth is not known, but what is known is that he died in 1434 after having

obtaining the manor of Brabourne, in what is now the
Ashford district of Kent, and building the family seat
of Scott's Hall, also referred to in some sources as
Scots Hall.

Other noted members of this family, who
held a number of high positions under a succession
of English monarchs, include Sir William Scott,
honorary Sword bearer to Henry V, who ruled from
1413 to 1422, and Sir Robert Scott, who is recorded
as having been Lieutenant of the Tower of London.

During the reign from 1461 to 1483 of
Edward IV, Sir John Scott was not only Comptroller
of the Royal Household but also Governor of Dover
Castle and Comptroller of Calais.

Under Henry VIII, his son Sir William Scott
also served as Governor of Dover Castle.

It is the Coat of Arms of this family that
features three Catherine wheels as its central motif
and crest of a demi-griffin, while mottoes include 'For
King and Country' and 'All good or nothing.'

Of a separate family of Scotts, Thomas Scott,
born in 1424 in Rotherham, Yorkshire, served as Lord
Chancellor of England; founder of Lincoln College,
Oxford, he died in 1500 after falling victim to the
plague.

Better known as the Duke of Monmouth, James Scott was at the centre of one of the most pivotal events in England's frequently turbulent history.

Born in 1649 in Rotterdam, the illegitimate son of Charles II, then living in exile, and his lover Lucy Walter, he was variously known as James Fitzroy or James Croft.

Created Duke of Monmouth after his father was restored to the throne in 1660, he married the heiress Anne Scott, 4th Countess of Buccleuch, and immediately adopted her surname.

Created Duke of Buccleuch in the Peerage of Scotland, in what is known as Monmouth's Rebellion he launched an abortive attempt to wrest the throne from the Catholic James II, who had succeeded Charles.

Exiled after James' accession to the throne, he landed at Lyme Regis, Dorset, on June 11 of 1685 and, with up to 4,000 armed supporters, captured Taunton, in Somerset.

But the rebellion was swiftly and brutally quelled when Monmouth was defeated by Royalist troops at Sedgemoor Hill on July 5.

The duke went into hiding but was captured

a short time later and, taken to London, executed on July 15.

His wife Anne, Duchess of Buccleuch, was able to retain her titles and estates.

In 1810, the 3rd Duke of Buccleuch inherited the Dukedom of Queensberry, meaning the present holder is only one of five people in the United Kingdom to hold two or more different dukedoms – in this case those of Monmouth, Buccleuch and Queensberry.

'Scott', meanwhile, remains their family name, while their family seats are Drumlanrig Castle, in Dumfries and Galloway, and Bowhill House, near Selkirk, in the Borders.

With other family properties that include Dalkeith Palace, Midlothian, Richard Scott, the 10th Duke, is the United Kingdom's largest private landholder, while he is also Chief of Clan Scott, whose motto is 'Love' and crest a stag.

Chapter three:

Exploration and the arts

One particularly intrepid bearer of the Scott name, and one who became a British national hero, was the Royal Navy officer and Antarctic explorer Captain Robert Falcon Scott.

Leader of two expeditions to the frozen wastes, it was while on the final one – to reach the South Pole – that he and four of his companions lost their lives.

Born in 1868 in Stoke Damerel, near Devonport, Devon, the third of six children, his father was a brewer and a magistrate.

The family, however, had strong military and naval traditions, and it was towards the latter that the young Scott was drawn, entering the naval training ship HMS *Britannia* when he was aged 13.

Qualifying as a midshipman two years later, he first went to sea aboard HMS *Boadicea*, flagship of the Cape Squadron.

Promoted to lieutenant in 1889, it was ten years later, while home on leave, that he met Sir Clements Markham, president of the Royal

Geographical Society (RGS) and whom he had first met several years before.

Markham was impressed by Scott and told him of an expedition to the Antarctic that the RGS planned.

Against some initial opposition from some quarters, Scott was chosen to be placed in overall command of what became the British National Antarctic Expedition – more famously known as the *Discovery* expedition.

Organised by the RGS and the scientific think-tank the Royal Society, it was staffed mainly by naval personnel such as Scott and also the explorer Ernest Shackleton.

Built in Dundee, their expedition vessel *Discovery* – more properly known as RRS *Discovery*, with 'RRS' denoting 'Royal Research Ship', was a three-masted wooden sailing ship with coal-fired auxiliary steam engines.

Fully fitted out and stocked with essential supplies, she set off for the inhospitable Antarctic waters in August of 1901.

The main aim of the expedition was not to reach the South Pole but to collect as much geological, zoological and biological findings as possible.

But the expedition was woefully unprepared – not least because of Scott's insistence on 'man-hauling' heavily laden sledges, in preference to the use of dogs that his Norwegian rival Roald Amundsen advocated, in addition to the use of skis.

On one early attempt at ice travel one of Scott's party, George Vine, was killed when he slipped over a precipice, while Shackleton had to abandon his part in the expedition through sheer physical exhaustion after having undertaken a trek with Edward Wilson.

The expedition spent two gruelling years on the ice, returning to Britain in September of 1904 and where Scott was lauded as a hero.

Promoted to the rank of captain, he was also made a Commander of the Royal Victorian Order (CVO).

He returned to full-time naval duties until, in 1910, he was placed in command of the *Terra Nova Expedition*, named from its ship, *Terra Nova*.

The RGS stated before the *Terra Nova* sailed that the main objective of the expedition was "scientific primarily, with exploration and the Pole as secondary objects."

Scott, however, aware that Amundsen was on

his way to attempt to reach the Pole, stated that as far as he was concerned his main objective was "to reach the South Pole, and to secure for the British Empire the honour of this achievement."

Along with four others – Henry Bowers, Edgar Evans, Lawrence Oates and Edward Wilson – Scott did indeed reach the Pole on January 12, 1912, but only to find Amundsen's party had beaten them to it by about five weeks.

Making their dispirited way back to base camp – exhausted, frozen and with their supplies all but depleted – Oates voluntarily left their tent and walked to his death with the farewell: "I am just going out and may be some time."

The rest of the party quickly succumbed to the terrible conditions, with Scott believed to have died on about March 29.

Their bodies were discovered by a search party on November 29, and buried where they had made camp.

In the years following the ill-fated *Terra Nova* expedition, a number of monuments and memorials were set up in honour of Scott while his first expedition vessel *Discovery*, now moored at Dundee's Discovery Point, is a major visitor attraction.

In 1908 meanwhile, Scott had married the sculptor and socialite Kathleen Bruce.

Their only child was the eminent conservationist, ornithologist, painter and sportsman Sir Peter Markham Scott.

Born in 1909 and a founder of the World Wide Fund for Nature and later a recipient of its prestigious gold medal, it was he who gave the scientific name Nessitera Rhombopteryx to the mysterious Loch Ness Monster, in order that it could be registered as an endangered species.

The name means "the monster of Ness with the diamond-shaped fin", and was based on an underwater photograph that showed a supposed fin.

Also representing Britain in sailing at the 1936 Berlin Olympics, he won a bronze medal in the O-Jolie dinghy class.

Knighted in 1973 for his contribution to the conservation of wild animals, he died in 1989.

His wife, Phillipa Scott (née Talbot-Ponsonby), was the conservationist and wildlife photographer born in 1918 in Bloemfontein, South Africa.

Honorary director of the Wildfowl and Wetlands Trust that was founded by her husband in

1948 and an associate of the Royal Photographic Society, she died in 2010.

One of the greatest literary figures of the late eighteenth and nineteenth centuries, Sir Walter Scott was the poet, playwright and historical novelist born in Edinburgh in 1771.

Practising for a time as a lawyer in his native city, he had been fascinated from an early age with his nation's rich and vibrant history, particularly that of the Borders, where his family hailed from and also had distant connections with the Scotts of Buccleuch.

Turning to full-time writing, his set of collected ballads, *The Minstrelsy of the Scottish Borders*, was published in 1796, followed by highly popular historical novels that include the *Waverley* novels and his *Tales of My Landlord* collection – that include his 1816 *Old Mortality* and, from 1818, *The Heart of Midlothian*.

Married in 1797 to French-born Genevieve Charpentier, he built a family home on the south bank of the River Tweed, near Melrose in his beloved Borders country.

Naming it Abbotsford, he added to it over the following years to leave what is now the major visitor attraction of Abbotsford House.

He was struck by financial disaster in 1825 when a nation-wide banking crisis led to the collapse of the Bannatyne printing business, leaving him liable for debts of a staggering £130,000.

Refusing offers of financial aid from friends and admirers, he determined to 'write' his way out of debt and, already in failing health, went on to produce other best-selling novels that include his 1826 *Woodstock* and his 1828 *The Fair Maid of Perth*.

It was only a short time after his death in 1832, thanks to the continuing success of his literary output, that his debts were finally discharged.

He was buried in Melrose Abbey, while the many memorials to him across the world include the imposing Scott Monument in Edinburgh's Princes Street and statues in both Glasgow's George Square and New York's Central Park.

Chapter four:

On the world stage

Born in Orange County, Virginia in 1898 to parents of Scots-American descent, George Randolph Scott was the veteran Hollywood actor better known as Randolph Scott.

Serving in France during the First World War as an artillery observer in the United States Army, it was not until 1927, nine years after the conflict ended, that he decided to pursue a career in the film industry.

His father, an engineer, was an acquaintance of fellow engineer, tycoon, aviator and film mogul Howard Hughes.

Providing his son with a letter of introduction to Hughes, the eccentric millionaire gave him a small role in the 1928 film *Sharp Shooters*.

Over the next 34 years he starred in a number of films, mainly the Westerns for which he is particularly remembered, although he also appeared in a number of other genres that include crime dramas and comedies.

Major film credits include the 1932 *Heritage of the Desert*, a number of Westerns based on the novels of Zane Grey, the 1936 *Follow the Fleet*, the 1941 *Belle Star* and, starring beside Marlene Dietrich and John Wayne, the 1955 *The Spoilers*.

The recipient of a star on the Hollywood Walk of Fame and an inductee of the Western Performers Hall of Fame at the National Cowboy and Western Heritage Museum in Oklahoma City, he died in 1987.

The first actor to reject an Academy Award for Best Actor, George Campbell Scott, better known as **George C. Scott**, was born in 1927 in Wise, Virginia.

It was for his portrayal of World War II American general George S. Patton in the 1970 *Patton* that he was nominated for the award. Despite refusing the nomination on the grounds that 'every great dramatic performance was unique and could not be compared to others', he nevertheless won the award – which is now on display in the museum of the Virginia Military Institute, which General Patton had attended.

Also a noted stage actor, rising to prominence in the 1950s for his roles in Shakespeare's *As You Like It* and Richard III, other major film credits include the role of General Buck Turgidson in the 1964 *Dr Strangelove*, the 1980 *The Changeling* and, from 1981, *Taps*.

He died in 1999, while he was the father through his marriage to the actress Colleen Dewhurst of the actor, producer, director and voice artist **Campbell Scott**.

Born in 1961 in New York City, he starred in the 1990 film *Longtime Companion*, the 1991 *Dying Companion* – in which his mother also appears – and the 2012 *The Amazing Spider-Man*.

A distant descendant of George Washington, 1st President of the United States, **Zachary Scott** was the actor noted for his roles of villains and scoundrels.

Born in 1914 in Austin, Texas, he appeared on the Broadway stage before making his film debut in the 1944 *The Mask of Dimitrios*, followed a year later and starring beside Joan Crawford, in *Mildred Pierce*.

He died in 1965, with other film credits that include the 1949 *Flamingo Road*, the 1950 *Shadow on the Wall* and, from 1960, *The Young One*.

An actress of both television and the big screen, **Jacqueline Sue Scott** was born in 1932 in Sikeston, Missouri. Television credits include *Perry Mason* and, from 1964 to 1967, *The Fugitive*, in the role of fugitive Dr Richard Kimble's sister, while film credits include the 1968 *Firecreek*, the 1971 *Duel* and, from 1977, *Telefon*.

Best known for his role of Steve Stifler in the *American Pie* series of films, including the 2012 *American Reunion*, **Seann Scott** is the actor born in 1976 in Cottage Grove, Minnesota.

Other film credits include the 2000 *Final Destination*, the 2005 *The Dukes of Hazzard* and, from 2011, *Goon*.

Beginning her media career with the Scottish newspaper *The Sunday Post* followed by working as a press officer for the tourist board for the Isle of Bute, **Selina Scott** is the journalist, newsreader, television producer and presenter born in 1951 in Scarborough, North Riding of Yorkshire.

Hired as a reporter and presenter with Grampian TV in 1978, she came to national attention two years later as a newsreader on ITV's *News at Ten*.

Joining the BBC's *Breakfast Time* programme in 1983, she later presented shows that include *The Clothes Show* before moving to the satellite channel Sky.

She has since produced a number of television documentaries on European royal figures who include Prince Charles and King Juan Carlos of Spain.

Behind the camera lens, **Ridley Scott** is the director and producer who received a knighthood in

2003 for his contribution to the British film industry. Born in 1937 in South Shields, Tyne and Wear, he was nominated for Academy Awards for Directing for his 1991 *Thelma and Louise*, the 2000 *Gladiator* and the 2001 *Black Hawk Down*.

Other noted works include the 1979 *Alien*, the 2005 *Kingdom of Heaven*, the 2007 *Prometheus* and the 2013 *The Counsellor*.

He is the older brother of the late film producer and director **Tony Scott**, born in 1944.

The recipient in 2008, along with his brother Ridley, of the BAFTA Britannia Award for Worldwide Contribution to Filmed Entertainment, his films include the 1983 *The Hunger*, the 1986 *Top Gun*, the 1995 *Crimson Tide* and the 2010 *Unstoppable*.

He committed suicide in August of 2012 by jumping from a bridge in San Pedro, California.

Bearers of the Scott name have also excelled, and continue to excel, in the highly competitive world of sport.

On the golf course, **Adam Scott** is the Australian golfer and player on the Professional Golfers Association (PGA) Tour who was runner-up to South African Ernie Els in the 2012 Open Championship.

Born in Adelaide in 1980, he was winner of the 2004 Players Championship and the 2013 Masters Tournament.

From golf to the skating rink, **Barbara Ann Scott King** – with 'King' her married name – was the Canadian figure skater who won the gold medal in the ladies' singles event at the 1948 Olympics.

Born in Ottawa in 1928 and world champion in 1947 and 1948, she also held the Canadian Figure Skating Championship from 1944 to 1946.

Known as "Canada's Sweetheart", she was the recipient of a number of honours that include being made an Officer of the Order of Canada, induction into the Canadian Olympic Hall of Fame and the International Women's Sports Hall of Fame; she died in 2012.

From sport to music, Ronald Belford Scott was the Scots-born vocalist with the Australian heavy rock band AC/DC better known as **Bon Scott**.

Born in Forfar in 1946 and raised in the small village of Kirriemuir, in Angus, he was aged six when his family immigrated to Australia, settling first in Melbourne and later in Fremantle.

Forming his own band, The Spektors, in 1965 and performing later with a number of other bands, it was in 1974 that he was chosen to replace Dave Evans as the lead singer of AC/DC. A number of internationally top-selling albums followed, including the 1976 *High Voltage* the 1977 *Let There Be Rock* and the 1979 *Highway to Hell*.

The vocalist died in 1980 after a night out in London, and has since been ranked at number one by *Classic Rock* magazine in a list of The 100 Greatest Frontmen Of All Time, while a stone slab commemorating him was unveiled in Kirriemuir in 2006.

In a much different musical genre, **Jill Scott** is the American singer, songwriter, poet and actress whose best-selling albums include her 2000 *Who Is Jill Scott?* Born in 1972, her television credits include the joint BBC/HBO series *The No. 1 Ladies' Detective Agency*, based on the novels by Alexander McCall Smith, and film credits that include the 2007 *Why Did I Get Married?*

Winner of the 2007 Americana Music Association's Song of the Year Award for his song *Hank Williams' Ghost*, **Darrell Scott** is the singer, songwriter and multi-instrumentalist born in 1959 in London, Kentucky. Along with Led Zeppelin vocalist Robert Plant, he has also performed with the group Band of Joy, playing instruments ranging from guitar and banjo to mandolin and accordion.

In the equally creative world of literature, **Duncan Campbell Scott**, born in Ottawa in 1862, was the Canadian poet and prose writer recognised, along with Bliss Carman, Archibald Lampman and Charles G. D. Roberts, as one of Canada's acclaimed Confederation Poets.

With poetry collections that include *The Magic House and Other Poems* and the 1916 *Lundy's Lane and Other Poems*, he was elected a Fellow of the Royal Society of Canada in 1889 and later served for a time as its president. The recipient of the society's prestigious Lord Pierce Medal for his contribution to Canadian literature, he died in 1947.

Taking to the heavens, David Randolph Scott, better known as **Dave Scott**, is the American engineer, former astronaut, retired U.S. Air Force officer and former test pilot who made his first space flight as pilot of the March 1966 *Gemini 8* mission, along with Neil Armstrong.

As commander of the 1971 *Apollo 15* mission, the fourth human lunar landing, he became the seventh person to walk on the Moon and the first to drive a vehicle on its surface.

Born in 1932 at the Randolph Field airbase – from which his middle name derives – he is the recipient of a number of honours and awards that include two NASA Distinguished Service Medals, the NASA Exceptional Service Medal and the Distinguished Flying Cross.

One particularly colourful, but ultimately tragic, bearer of the proud name of Scott was the American daredevil Samuel Gilbert Scott, better known as **Sam Scott**.

Born in about 1813 in Philadelphia, it was while serving in the United States Navy that he became renowned for his dangerous stunt of diving from the masts of naval vessels into the depths of the sea. Becoming a professional stuntman, he performed other daring acts involving diving or jumping from great heights, including one from a precipice near Niagara Falls.

But his dangerous career came to a decidedly abrupt end on January 11, 1841 while on a visit to England. This was when, planning to jump from scaffolding that had been especially erected for him on London's Waterloo Bridge and into the waters of the Thames, he became entangled in a rope on which he was swinging and was accidently hanged – to the horror of the hundreds of spectators who had come to witness the American daredevil in action.